CW00850655

RANDOM PROSE

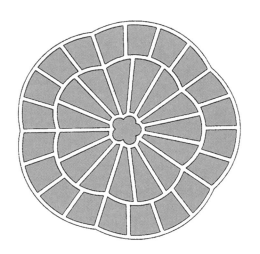

RANDOM PROSE

IZZAT MAJEED

QUARTET

First published in 2010 by
Quartet Books Limited
A member of the Namara Group
27 Goodge Street, London W1T 2LD

A catalogue record for this book
is available from the British Library

ISBN   978 0 7043 7203 0

Typeset in Great Britain by Antony Gray
Printed and bound by
T J International Ltd, Padstow, Cornwall

1

let not this fitful fever i have
scare you into the conformity of wasting away
on satin pillows and corporate deadlines
    and self-congratulatory recipes in the kitchen —

it is contagious i know
the smugness of affluence
the camouflaged mediocrity
the ordinariness parading as celebrity of this or that kind —

let not the toss of debased coins carry the illusion
of gods rearranging stars just because you think they ought to
they don't you know
not this dreamer of a perfectly orbiting planet love
nor the angry traveller strutting through black holes of angry messiahs
seeking one convenient dimension of belonging after another

let not these words go on and on
seize at least one meaning one nuance one god
and lay back on unfashionable sofas
to reflect upon life's fever
and love's core

2

bring chaos to your life dear heart
be a snowflake that leads to hurricanes
a long leaf falling from the learning tree
sighing away a sad knowledge that knows not
    the mystery of love

life is a walkabout in the wilderness of sunburnt logic
accumulated memories of needless pain
and dew-lived happiness

bring grave thoughts to our common sleep
and fear not the toll collectors of dreams
    they work for caesar
despair and repair not the day-worn look that you keep
hidden from me

3

kind-hearted woman
when you cross the gates of desire
do you look back to see if your hands are in mine
or do you rush to the ladder of longing
and climb into the fire of perchanced dreams
of just you and your rush to fate

wait
kind-hearted woman
these are percipient steps to love foretold
the star over jesus only kings could see
in the ocean of poverty
i am the kingdom of your heart
you are the sovereign of this realm
ranging from one corner of my heart to the other
larger than the milky way
and more in love than the breadth of this petty universe

4

now i go to sleep
       and take on the world
as in the deep of day

the sweep and stay of chequered steps
that lead the journey away
from all that matters in this heart of mine

now i toss and turn
to soothe the burn of angry eyes
thoughtless stars which do not budge astray
       from the orbit of fate

now i cross the strait
between the ocean of hope and the ocean of hope
gathering the wind in her hair
to sail the ship of my love's riches
and keep the north star of her look
always in the core of my sky

5

say
i do not believe in you
and then go home to all those idols of gold and honey
and try to find one that fulfils the rush
captivated in the lust of time falling in silver sands
of a hurried hourglass of elapsed eternity
                          in the palm of your hands

say
unbeliever you
i too have my own pantheon lost in the mist of tears
come and go as you please on the chessboard of frozen pawns
nothing will move in the garrisons of your new found allies
hellos and feasts and the sharing of plundered loot
                          from my heart's defeat

say
this love i stumbled upon saved the day
in all the days of my life
and made the night
into the bright gift of bride moon
inconstant
yet mine
you and the full moon

6

betray me as you will
      in the spill of stars
rushing through ravished promises of a fickle life

half a moon is half a moon still
      half a sun is not
half a love is a barren world
      that once sounded so fulfilled

betray me as you will
      in the shrill of hurly-burly success
the work and play of someone else's days and heavy nights
that will go away
      as will the children of our love
and in the silence of the chill
      a sinking heart and a mind on fire
will betray all your calculations
how then will you forget that it is i
who remains the truth of all that we have
and all that we don't

7

talk to me when the noise and the rush of forced journeys
           abate
when digital people turn away and you begin to see
your face in plasma screens
when you sit alone in the courtyard of friends
and call out to one above all when you think of being one
with the other

today
the laser-etched labyrinth of life
takes you at the speed of light to a heartless cyber space
           of paper wealth and faceless people
think of me when you turn the page of a real book
and smile at poets when you look in their eyes
and tell them you know one even though you don't much like poetry
(not the modern kind anyway – it makes no sense)

betray not the real password to my heart
           (the one only you know)
and let not your impatience with life hack a way
into the programme of my love

8

i live a life
i let go dreams when they don't come true
other people too
i let the clouds sing to me
in zephyr's song
a drunken breeze dancing with eager trees
paints my face with the elixir of dying forests

i find life in long lost ways
recently excavated cities in her eyes
i have time's brush tenderly clearing the sad sands of broken hourglasses
i blow softly on wounded paintings of her lament
i bandage hearts waylaid by heartless roads

i live life
life does not live me
i give of myself at every turn of pain
i gain nothing from sunken galleons of looted joy
i remain alive by calling out to you
and you i know cannot but hear me

9

between the real and the imagined
      (or the imagined and the real)
there is a bridge of belonging
      the inconvenience of longing for the other
however distant
      unattainable
a journey difficult in the ease with which it is undertaken

so come shakuntala
woman of green earth and smiling ripples of streams that become rivers
undress the mysteries of the sanctuaries we know not
henna havens deep in the lines of the lord's dance on your palms
unclothe your fears in the heart of the metropolis
and announce the marriage of the real and the imagined
to the applause of lost loves and the only one that matters
bread and butter and rum and romance of every forced encounter
the stutter of a broken hurrah
when a quiet exit on the chariot of tears would have been fine
come shakuntala
let me herald your name in the hearts of other goddesses
      of other gods

hurry shakuntala
        for i fear
by the time you declare what i mean to you
i will be the fallen idol in the ravine of abandoned promises
and you will have been taken prisoner by the road not taken

10

two score years and ten
a pun on when it is half gone
then
three score years and ten
the magic flute playing the pied piper of times past
the piety of lust and the holier-than-thou chants
        of trader monks and broken dervishes
a craving for chocolate encounters with half-deciphered women
books abandoned in mid-page
        rediscovered in age
reinvented in the rage of time's prison

life is all about metaphor and the idioms of the present
'for what doth it profit a man' . . . and all that
let there be light in what is left of darkness
give me peace in the agony of faith
time
mother earth in the slingshot of creation
give me the season of love and half a loaf of bread

11

is it the flame in the temple or the temple in the flame
is it the monk in denial or the denial in the monk
is it the player in the game or the game in the player
is it the hunt of the hungry or the hunger in the hunt
is it the want in plenty or the plenty in want
is it the dream in a sleep or a sleep in the dream
is it the stream in the river or the river in the stream
is it the dance of time or the time of dance
is it you in eternity or eternity in you
is it the breeze in the garden or the garden in the breeze
is it the anguish in knowing or the knowing in anguish
is it the illusion in happiness or the happiness in illusion
is it the moon in your eyes or your eyes in the moon
is it just a play on words or is it the word in play

12

she can be as fickle and as steadfast
            as the firefly and the north star
restless as a pillowless tossing and turning
soft hum of a long forgotten song
she is the curator of dreams
the archaeologist of sleep
she is the discoverer of life's lost civilisation
the machete cutting through snakes of eden
and the keeper of the rainforest of silent tears
she is the ever ready bandage of unnecessary wounds
the great forgiver of innocent hurt
builder of tomorrow's bricks and the mother of the day after
she revives the memory of great vows
from blood on blood to destiny and distinction
she is the maya and the mughal of the heart's history
she is the story i keep telling myself
she is the roomful of lullaby candles as if there is no other right

13

make something else out of this world
show me the dance of andalus in the daily commute
give me the song of the indus you wrote and then forgot
make me the beginning of time with a watch
      that works only when i want it to
as it is this world just is

make something else out of this world
take the ordinary and fill it with the magic of what was lost
when we did not make something else out of this world

ebb tides and ordinary shores and bland weather
make brave storms and symphonic rain and playful oceans
the bane of stale encounters and hollow hellos
give me the awe and wonder of knowing
      the other in my ordinariness
make me understand all conversations with your heart
and let me help you make something else out of this world

14

i offer you simple and splendid love
riveting anchors of a real person
i offer you shelter from the cloning of your reflections
resplendent castles in the heartland of fairytales come true
i offer you peace when coward fears declare war
the company of one greater than the fuss and clutter of passers-by
i offer you a friend as no other
a loyal subject of my own heart i gave to you
i offer you words that mean more than they mean
truth and steadfastness and jealousy and faith
i offer you the grand alliance of passion and lust and togetherness
abandonment and helplessness and laughter and warm winter nights
i offer you tomorrow today
the joy and pain the hurt and heal and the offer

15

your thug heart waylays every journey i make
takes a treasure chest of chinese pearls of wisdom
the forebodings of my mind's oracle of delphi
the myrrh of ruin's swirl of surrender
and leaves me at kali's footsteps
          beneath the dance of her infinite hands

another journey
and the cossack rapiers of your eyes
come charging at the presence of distant villages
and the uncontrolled fires of rainless steppes
they lift the sensuous brides of my making and ravish them
with the freedom from the drudgery of making dough
and setting fire to their dreams

another journey
and your thug heart carries me away
          from the caravan of my words and letters
this time though i gather my breath and carry the message
          in the amulet of forbidden riches
read it o thug of my heart
it says all i think of in my steps of an odyssey
is to travel to you

16

if you fear a home in the clouds
come near and nearer still
and i will show you the stairway to mount desire
each step a stage closer to the theatre of wishes
with an audience of one
and the fulfilment of knowing that this one
is all the applause of the heart
and all the thrill of that first step

if you slip on the grime of survival
(daily bread and tomorrow's dread)
let the real hunger for the other
make you fast on an empty stomach and a full heart
and then let us break our fast together
in a feast of the senses like no other

17

thinking of you eases the pain
of nothing making anything nothing again
bossa nova rhythms and morning ragas soothing the wrong time of day
vainglorious reflections of self-created beauty in borrowed mirror of light
          on loan from your eyes

wise dreams take flight at night
seeking to make the next day more than humdrum tick tocks
they create the days of the mind feeling busy in the grand escapes of thought
and give peace to the mihrab of my heart
          where i think of you

i used to worry
          if thinking of you made you think of me
not any more
because you will change if i cannot feel you thinking of me
and a changed you is not the one i would want to think about

thinking of you is great fun
          it is the sun
on the freezing cold on the green outside my window
it is the happy flock of birds resting in the warmth of my sight
it is the little breeze that barely shakes the branches of leafless trees
and reminds me to go out in the world
and declare a holiday from pain

18

when things change
      and you for example are not you any more
but what you thought you would be
if one of the roads that came your way
      beckoned you wholeheartedly
and you took it with all the fanfare of choices made
happy freedom along with grudgeless surrender
      the mix and match of make-believe stars
and the wages of the day
would you then take a wrinkled night
and iron it with the age of your hands
and fold the dawn in one corner of time
till you remembered again what it was
what it is
that keeps and kept the world alive
and the earth in the orbit of our hearts

19

let there be a famine
if it's just the crop of sadness
                that we harvest
cries and moans of victims of capricious seasons
the furrows of sighs
the stubborn plough of wood
                from the tree of salvation
in the arrogant field of consumed wishes

give me the overflowing silos of plenty
a single grain of happiness escaping the shelter
                of charity and largesse of overfed gods
a year's supply of assured love
fill the next failed monsoon
and the next angry dawn

20

have you been to the other earth
        deep inside the mind of the universe
she too was born with the one you know
same history – same people – same dreams – same moment – same chaos

have you seen us you and i
        looking at the same sky
wondering if we also exist on the other side of this reality
do you see me wanting to be with you
here and now and in all dimensions
        of longing and surrender and care
can you not feel that you and i will always be one
on this earth that pains us so
and on the other that pains us so
on this mother earth that gives us our you and i
and on the other that gives us
        what we choose to make of this
our life together

21

so once she reads it
       is the poem dead
words read in an all too familiar patronage
where then are they lodged
these alphabets of rhyme and song
where do i find them ever again
and who cares once the flavour is licked
              dry off this page

work in progress
this
and the other couldn't care less

22

yes there are concerns and sighs and laments
and the business of surviving each day
with enough crop of hope in the harvest of night
and the counting of blessings and the fear of losing them
(one by one or all at once)
and having faith in the heart's keeper and keeping it alive
in the age in which the joy of anything is lost in the race to nothing
and the yearning for what is not
and the forgetting of what is and remains
and the taking for granted the round-the-corner embrace
the hug the sheltering arms the hair-combing fingers
the cupped hands carrying water across the lips of thirst
and the urge to sing out a song for no reason at all
and the coup de coeur at each settled moment
on the rocking chair of denial and dead movement
and the thrift of praise for the loved one
and forgetting that love cannot be stored in any sense in my love
it must be given to the other all the time
in every blink of waking life and in every turn of restless sleep

23

be a dreamer be
see all the illusions in the sea of possibility
let them belie the rainbow colours
let the words stick to your lips
      unwilling to part
from a lexicon of one language you have given to me

be a lexis be
fallow words awaiting the plough of my pen . . .
the nexus of hordes in love
conquering your heart with mongol ease

be a warrior be
silk helmets and shields of caresses
come to the defence of hope and lust
in every look of advancing care
in every feel of victorious touch

24

there is a whole universe in my heart
      the big bang of laying my eyes upon you
instantly creating galaxies of desire and passion
and thought and music and words and abandonment
to the forces of mystery and awe and pure beauty

black holes of travelling to another dimension of the present
another corner of the heart in turmoil with expanding space
which is created only to be filled with your existence
another journey with no tomorrow and with all my yesterdays
leading to the significance of only that which is what i behold

dying stars make me see what they give birth to:
the heart and dust of many suns breaking promises with another day
a night
light years long waiting for that one full moon
      i see in your face
and in all the swirl of time and intellect
my heart is a universe
      filled by your presence
      and the thought of you

25

think of it this way
        fate
        is another day
        gone by
it is the laughter and the hurt of the past
        travels to another heart
a resting place in caravanserais
amidst mongol armies conquering dreams of another love
wearing the armour of silk facing arrows of gold

pity the downtrodden future
        oppressed already before its birth
why not make a feast of the present
garnished with moments
and moments and moments
calling out to the keeper of time
and saying enough to the dance of the hourglass

come sweet today and stay
the guardian of my faith in you

26

where does the mind's eye rest
when you think of me in love
or love or the future or the very now
or how the others look at you and perhaps if they
look at you the way you want them to
or think of you the way you think they ought to
or just worry about money and things and institutions
and time and age and wrinkles and aches and pains
or just cry damn it all and bring forth the courage
which is after all the other name of being in love to the very end

why do you want the heart's prose to be anything less
than these words of just everyday belonging
this here is the silky secret of it all
(hackneyed as it may sound though in fact it is always a fresh wound)
there is nothing more to it
the mind's eye – the heart's prose or rhyme
is all joy in all the shades
when you think of me
when i think of you

27

i have washed the sun for you
       polished the full moon
i have bottled the angry oceans
       imprisoned the gods in statues of clay
i have turned coal into diamonds
       sands to monuments of eternal love
i have folded the sky neatly into the pocket of adoration
stitched the clouds with the thread of rainbows
       to give you shelter in the shade of all the colours

i have rubbed mountains into kohl
i have made henna out of forgotten forests of life
i have made fireflies out of shooting stars
       and set them free in your hair

i have made myself at one with you
why do you then fear the sun and the moon
why do you then not have faith in all the stars
       i have in the palm of my hand

28

fall in love with me again
or did we just fall in love in this treasure of two score years
and the vicinity of pain and memory
give or take an experience or two
make or break the past at will
only to set free the passion in us
the compassion for you the lust
the tingling pores awakened to that touch
this breathe of longing
and how does it make any sense to consume
each other
why not be the ability of the other to give strength
eyelashes braided together in the mind
the heart's ships sailing with all the cargoes
of carefree todays and this moment
you and i have together
so what's the hurry

29

half a heart is no heart
half a pain is no pain

half a journey is not the first step
half a pebble does not a shore make

half a battle is a battle lost
half a war is still one half to end

half a grain is just more hunger
half a rain is half a river

half a kiss does not moisten the lips
half an embrace brings the cold in

half a tear dries in its own salt
half a whisper is stolen by its own breath

half a flame is half a flame
half a night is tame and dark

half a moon is just anticipation
half a love is one half of nothing

30

you are
what the stars dealt to me
who am i
          to quarrel with that
who am i to go around the sun
unless
i am your planet of passion
unless
i am the orbit of pain
unless
i am the salvation of today
the here and now of helplessness

31

you are my essence
    you are my tears
    you are my fears
you are all i hear
you are all i see
you are my heart
you are my start
you are my beginning
you are my end
you are the plough
    i am the earth
you are the sweat
    i am the harvest
you are the end of regret
you are the death of lament
you are the sweet sleep
you are the day's work

32

say goodbye to the dream
      that perfect sleep within the sleep
make all the thick-tongued excuses to walk away
      in a sleepwalker's game of hide and seek
accuse your own paradise lost
of having waylaid the treasure trove of smiles
and then when you wake up
go to work
find a new home and immediately realise
they are the same walls
these are the same ashes of all the blossoms
      that were there to last and last
and then go to sleep again
for it is in that dream that you have that we live

33

to the tune of a long forgotten song

you got it wrong girl
        there is no right
if right is all you seek
        there is no wrong
if wrong is all you see

you got it bad girl
        there is no good in reality
if the real is all you have
there is no bad in wanting it all
        if wanting it all is all you want

you got it sad girl
        don't close the cotton club of your heart
it's where we meet blues and all
it's where we dance to the escaped music of our love

34

why burn a candle when the sun is out
either let the flame be your light
or dim the sun into the greys of life's ifs and buts
or wait for the full moon and bathe your eyes in reflected glory
and let soft moonbeams soothe the fury of a star on fire

why fall for the call of a full moon
    helpless howlings – bleeding dreams
oceans swelling like a beloved's heart in your hands

let the night rein in the rhythms of distant ruffles
and dance tiptoe upon tiptoe slowly slowly
away from the crowd of afflictions

here then is the setting:
one life half gone with no memory just fear of the present
or one life just beginning with the moon in one hand and the sun in the other
and a flame so bright that comes alive
at every thought of the loved one
making a poor flicker of all the suns in heaven
and carrying the full moon in one tear of separation

35

love is a strange emotion
      it seeks renewal and reassurance
where none is required
it begs: tell me you love me
and then it asks: do you love me more than ever before
and then it says: you are mine for ever

and then you descend into quotidian hell
and pretend that not answering the call of love
is a controlled response to an otherwise dangerous allegiance

love is a strange planet
it is loyal to its own sun glowing in its own heart
and it is true to an orbit of surrender
to a received feeling of how much one is loved
but still asks: do you love me
o centre of my tossing and turning
tell me you love me
say it is above all else in the labyrinth of possession
just keep the words 'i love you'
      in the heart of a kiss
and in those eyes that always need to know
how much you love me

36

a sense of sacrifice
a fleeting grip on happiness on the way to belonging
a festival of giving of your self
a quietness in not having the dream become flesh
a fever of passion that never lets go
a sea of compassion for the other
a madness that is all too free
a sadness that says yes to life
a realm of the senses on the rampage
a coronation of hope
a softness breaking the glare of a harsh look
a celebration of every turn of the earth

the evanescence of pain in just one touch
the mellow melancholy of sighs that reassure
the acronyms of love no other can understand
the lighthouse on the rock of a new-found land
the conversion to the faith of your own making
the call to prayers when the eyes meet
the perpetual trade fair of vows
the never-ending happy pilgrimage to your heart
the simple truth of being together

this my love is love

37

nothing is really important in this life
      or in the one imagined within it
nothing really escapes from eyes contemplating eyes
when they go hard looking at just one view
      from a half-climbed hill

nothing really matters unless you want it to
and then everything matters to a point where it sticks
to the soles of your feet and questions
      every step you take

you tell me that it matters
      and i believe you
but then belief
      and all that matters
and all there is
      is
and that is all that matters

38

when it's all done
when the sun sets for the last time
when the moon betrays night
when the morning breeze burns the garden
when the road bends into the river in flood
when the thatched roofs soak up the monsoon
when fickle flames light up blank pages defying rhyme
when a tired peasant ploughs his own grave
when a forced harvest of rushed pain yields nothing but pain
when the whole surrenders to rebellious parts in the arrogance of fashion
when lonely people seek nothing but a kind word from a passer-by
when a failed dream comes again and again and you don't remember
when the scheme of things unfolds into just the things you don't want
when grand ideas and a hefty bank account go hand in hand
when the stock of truth and the equity of love crashes
when the index of passion becomes dried ink on a forgotten page:

will you leave me a message in love
and not forget what it means just for this lifetime

39

looking out the window
lamp-posts swaying in the mood of light
trees in half-dance
lost in the brave symphony of leaves
forgetting they too would falter and fall
into the oven of renewal
and bake every season with the fire of your promise

i wait for a garland caesar-bound
and quietly whisper to sister breeze:
this grand parade of love
on the great boulevard of my heart
celebrates anniversaries in heartbeats
        and not in distant time
every time my heart beats
it brings in a new season outside my window

40

spent the whole day
working to create a dream
i would dream in a dream
in my sleep at night
another day
another dream
another night

41

the stuff of memory
on the edge of tentativeness
should i delve into it
or will you be my mirror for ever
here
the geometry of reflections
there
the calculus of incalculable
helplessness

42

this heart is two thirds water one third earth
now the tiny springs swell into the pain of oceans
now mother earth remembers the love she had for the loved one
earth and water
tears and the sands of another time on the sundial of another heart
yours and mine
this business of the heart can be truly heartless
if you go into the fractions of love and niggardly passion
as if my heart can find an orbit
other than the one i myself have chiselled
with the help of your eyes
and the sun you let out when you look at me and smile

43

she crept into my heart
and stole the first caravan of frankincense
                        and sundried dreams
to bring back the fragrance
                        of an escaped fate
to the senses of a sense of loss
and a feeling of stealth crowning
the euphoria of a raid on the riches
of sudden blossoms in a desert
and strange pickings in a meadow of clouds

44

you occupy me at the core of my intellect
           the construction-site of words
the rules of an unread grammar of living
           i seem to master with you

you make me think about the meaning
           of small gestures of care and the nourishment
           of fingertips on the windowpane of the heart

you make me not care
           about things that don't need caring:
possessions and riches and fancy icons

you make me say out loud:
here
on this paper
is all the freedom and all the peace
i have found because you sit beside me
and help me make the world worth our while

45

don't break rank with the procession of passion
dead-end alleys are no escape
            from the slogans of comrade heart
and the stone-throwing rebellion of a burning mind

duende
guitar rhythms of sensual enticements
bacchic glory of abandon and shouting out loud
            the anthem of our lovehood

duende
gypsy wanderings across flamenco time
on the heels of solid taps on the floor of our hands

duende
the music i hear
moves away from around-the-corner homelessness
and at every turn of the road
            in this city where we live
i remain the cheer of the dance of us
the whole gathering of applause
            from the procession of passion
the entire roar of affirmation of our love

46

a sunbeam breaks through a dark cloud
this cloud will close the window of light
or the sun will come out

not for long
       the armada of dark clouds
sailing in assumed victory across an inverted sea of the sky
       not for long
the cool sunshine of silken moods
       half betrayed into happiness
       half surrendered to the absence and the wait

i have you
to make the dark clouds become our benign monsoon
i have you
to keep the flame greater than the sun
light up the festival of the heart
i have you
to play hide and seek with all illusions
with your eyes clearing the dense of an opaque sky
i have you
to hold me when the sun goes out in the day
i have you
when the full moon sets the mind free at full tide

47

speak to me in the whisper castles of your mind
let down the drawbridge of our journey on your own
and come nimble footed into the silences of our realm

i will fill the moat of your day's labour
            with the stuff of mother earth
that will become the garden of all the blossoms
you seek in your seasons of dread
and untended balconies
where you think you live alone

48

could it be
        that you love me
because there is nothing else to do
loves that were not
        people who forgot their way
in the labyrinth of the heart
ghouls and knaves who ran away
        to put on the masks of wronged angels

robbers of graves of hurried revolutions
        no heroes – no icons – no ideas
dying passions in the wake of just dying
i should have loved you when i was at the barricades
perhaps then i would have known what this struggle is all about
would you have loved me in the golgotha of fallen dreams
would you have recognised me then
and do you see me now as the love that is just there
or do you feel the need to love me
as much as you need to breathe

49

beware
every smile
that comes to your lips
is in the wake of a tear
that wipes it off

50

the same questions
the same answers
i don't understand the questions
i don't have the answers
all i know is all of you
all i give is all of me

51

in her sleep she visited me
with the famine in the world of plenty
and the drought of compassion in the apathy of affluence
she said:
would we have loved under a dead sky
and would you have remembered my beauty
beneath the torn fabric of my once translucent skin
would you have kissed me with the lips of hunger
       and the dried blood on the scales of not knowing why
would you have carried me to the tins of handouts
and un–needed bandages i would have eaten
on the way back to the memory of when you first touched my eyes

in her sleep
i wake up and rush to the mirror
and i see how much i love her
       because i must and i can
and i turn to her as she turns in her sleep in wonder
and i tell her that all i know is all i see
in every hunger
and in the not knowing why

52

come great words
bring the troupe of hungry lyricism
to the life's stage of my audience of one
and let her cut through the razzle-dazzle
                                    of wordplay
only to applaud the effort i make
to give her the word of my flesh
sentient to all the real journeys she makes
                        to my broken alleys
in the walled city of her citizen dreams

come my words to the lips of her smile
and become ever healing in the balm
of love's hurt

53

any and every book
　　　　i have loved in life
has your name in it
　　　　i read again and again
the rubáiyát of khayyám
contemplating the snakes and ladders of fateful stars
and that one moment with you when it all begins
the pain – the joy – the cry – the sigh
the whirl of care and longing
the moving finger writes our story with the ink of our soul
and moves on to a summer's day that is but a mirror to your face
sublime beauty and lustful mine
in all the words of rumi – neruda – a fresh line
of metaphors falling from your eyes
why unweave the fabric of the heart's loom
look at the words of the mind's leaves
hanging on the pages of any and every book
　　　　i have loved in life
to seek you out at every turn of meaning
inside the swirl of rhyme
just you – a book – a glass of wine

54

let us count our blessings
       lesser mortals we
              you and i:
we are one in our soul
and we are alive
       if only when we are with each other
             together
and want nothing else
       you and i

55

not thinking of you
        is not a day
not a thought lost
in night-coloured curtains of one unfolding play
revived
not for any other audience except the one
made up of actors of not a forced life of clever lines
but of charmed words not given to the flourish of vain acclaim –

being
not with you
is a fault not of not being there
but of being with you
even when you are not there
and not for nothing is being together
a life of belonging
whether you like it or not –

56

how many heartaches of mine will you survive
this one at the end of silence
had journeyed to the feel of my fingertips
and in the scare of being paralysed with emotion
seeks a reprieve from pain and just wants to give you
the rhythm of the dance of my heart beating
in the same breath as the percussion of your eyes blinking
(moist and mine)
your feet ploughing the fields of my senses
with the crop of festive harvests
and reaping the beat of distant hope
making music in the rustle of a friendly forest
and the campfire of life and love
around the crackle of all the sparks that light the night
and show my heartache the healer in you –

57

step out of the culture of reflections
　　　they weave a spell of embellishments
around brittle self-worship
and leave out the reality of simple truths and complete love –
there are days without the other
these are nights with demon surrender to the ordinary
nitty-gritty accounting of unprovoked denial
shifting allegiances of friends of the heart
fickle longing that leaps to the comfort
of a tired bed of paper roses
　　　　　and cardboard saints of passion –
just one candle is enough
look into the flame and burn the dream slowly
this one brave fire will see you through
the tentative steps you take towards
　　　the leap of faith –

58

these dreams never are
                  but always stay
                         away
                 from reality
nay
    the sheer burn of phantom escapes
      the ever unsuccessful grain of today
slipping towards the wrong end of the hourglass

these true reflections of a serene affirmation
    concocting the potions of sleep
           just before our brave encounters with daybreaks
they all must unearth life in our private history:

    the rise and fall of the empire of hope
    the great reign of time spent together
and the abdication of one dream for another
    the coronation of our love in the unfinished cathedral of the heart
and the spectacle of all those gladiatorial moments
    when you and i refused a crown
and went away as ordinary citizens of a land that is all of us —

59

henna decorates into the palms of my hands
　　　　and is still not dry
will you not then − love of all loves −
　　comb my hair with your fingers
what colour is this
　　　　blood and the mud of my body
the green of renewal resting resplendently
in the hue of that colour of sunset i know and know not −
see how this henna fills the furrows of fate
see how these hands make a painting of our miniature cosmos
the hide and seek of where i am and where
the pull of your ever new-born sun sets the orbit −
comb my hair with your fingers
　　　　　　　　　love of all loves
i will not touch them
i will not let this henna dry as long as you are there
i will not give names to these colours of my love −

60

public truths and private lies
private lives and public cries
public myths and private faith
private prayers and public sighs

public sun and private moon
private heart and public doom
public mimes and private shadows
private valleys and public meadows
public rhymes and private chaos
private times and public pathos
public blues and private meanings
private muses and public gleanings
public past and private present
private past and public present

private truths and public lies
public lives and private cries
private myths and public faith
public prayers and private sighs

61

i have seen the temples of mighty aspirations and capricious oracles
    bathed in the blood of fresh dreams
half soaked in the lust of this or that god's golden reflections
i have stood at altars where virgin wonderment is sacrificed
and vesper shadows hide vestal fires in new vessels of our own making –
i have seen people break their own heart
    and then blame their own nothingness for doing nothing
a new religion of disbelief at every broken vow
a running away from heretic passions and the prophets of belonging –
i have seen the half-moon broken in two and no one believed me
i have taken tears to the river of clouds and made the rain of plenty
i have carved livelihood and the sins of contemplation
               in parthenons and ramparts of clay
i have spoken to my heart and this is what it says:
hail o loved one
i seek no temple but your arms
i hear no gods but your whispers
i see nothing but you –

62

words of hurt are words of hurt
once let loose they become scimitars
        of a conquering horde
of sad meanings and meaningless sadness –
so my love
the snow does not fall on the saharas of today
arid dreams do not water the oases of shifting sands
and a single palm tree has no shade
        in the heart of a noon sun
unless a partner palm sends a roof of protection
        against indifferent light and a burning skin –
travellers meet and caravans are born
        one love – one passion
is the silk route to the wealth of the soul
one hunger – a world of deprivations
is the manhattan of denial –
tread carefully in well-planned cities
        my love
these pyramids have no mystery
these pavements are lined with an alchemist's gold
these outstretched hands are tired now
it seems the words of hurt
have become and alms of love –

63

a little ache in the heart is good
they say it keeps the heartbreak away
some lament is always welcome
it shows what a greater loss would tear apart
a few broken dreams must be remembered
they make you see what it means to dream
a little absence keeps you going
for a complete union is the stuff of make believe
(blind faith is a blessing
        and blessed am i for i have blind faith in you) –
my little ache is as big as the world i live in
                it breaks my heart
just as i pretend to keep my heartbreak at bay
they say it is good to hurt a little
       they say – they say – they say
but i don't hear them any more

little aches and heartbreaks
here is a journey no one can make alone –

64

waylaid by her eyes
robbed of reason by just one whisper
she ambushes the seasons of my skies trapped
       in the hourglass – the ferris wheel
the furrows of this heart
wrinkled deep by the plough of her fingers
sowing her riches looted from temples of the impossible
       and oblivion –

this is a strange harvest this love
changing sallow ripenings to the vigour
       of her body's golden yield
look at her scythe through the wild outgrowth
  of hissing weeds of apathy and boredom in the land of plenty
look at her scour unseasonal sacraments and make sacred
the way she carries my eyes in her look –

65

this is a jar of unfinished poems
thoughts all of you
echoes of hesitant rhyme
half-contrived in a world of stony metres
afraid
half psalms of a spontaneous supplication
        to the wayward god of my heart –

these are notes to a fitful memory
creased first lines streaking across homeric horizons
where steadfast love simmers in the passion of the wait –

come ye words
give life to the union of fire and dreams
clothe me in her song
and let me complete this cycle of dance and death
come ye words
let us together possess her in all her meaning –

66

be faithful
     there are lives and loves to be lived in our oneness
(stubborn allegiances
         declarations of war
pacts to be kept in cordial hypocrisy)

be a convert to the religion of one love above all
one passion among lesser freedoms
one belonging beyond all missed tours of romance
one tryst with the midnight oil before the promise of dawn

be mine
and see the miracle of the here and now
     give you all of time
pick me in the crowd of choices
and announce me as your true companion
at the great feast of life
     the banquet of lost causes
the campfire of forgotten tribes

67

the meadow of lament
      this spring of tears
brings forth the crop of fears
i thought had been harvested before the last flood

mud slides and angry seasons
low clouds and blind flights
      of black swans and thief crows
stealing the ripening of our staple tomorrows –
needle peaks stitching the sky
      before the angels of wishes
fall through to the pull of the fall
and become human
      and then wish they were angels

look at the arrogant sun
      machiavellian full moon
the only escape from these ultimately wayward sprinklers of fate
is you
and the sun in your heart
and the full moon in your eyes

68

maya
       wealth and illusion
              or the wealth of illusion

kaam
       sensuality and lust
              beyond the animal

fikr
       thought, worry and despair
              the wear and tear of thinking of you

nirvan
       this worldliness with you
otherworldliness that becomes tangible
if you remain the companion across the river

maya – kaam – fikr – nirvan
       tell me what else is faith
when i see all this in you
       what more is love
              if not us

69

the elements don't care
   she's not there
and until she comes out of nowhere
the everywhere is a void
           no one can see

70

the architecture of everlasting lives
travelling through the bricks and mortar
                                   of simple silences
these are the newly discovered streets
        of the lost cities of the heart

i see you turn the corner and then wait
        with the garland of your smile
i run down the main road of our own festivals
and like a child
                a friend
                        the one love
i rush time and run to you
your happy fingers housed in the palm of my hand

71

i do not want to burn alone
in the mind's filigree of incandescent four walls
and suffer the gaze of passing eyes
the salute of artisans chained to marble
     and their chiselled dreams
leave me cold in a dying flame
     gasping for breath surrounded by so much beauty

would you not then be my promethean love
     i promise i will offer my body to the gods
when the gnawing punishment falls on you
     for stealing the fire from my mind and offering it to my heart

i intervene and cry out loud:
     she is the flame i carry
          in all the opulence of this world
she is the love of my inner treasure
she is the liberator of my infatuation with greed
she is the reason for my thirst for knowledge
she is the only one who can see through
filigree frills of the mind

she is the only one
who can make a taj mahal in my heart

72

o candle burn bright
she awakes in the dark
with all light still trapped in her dream-sun
and all her shimmer of resolve is like broken mercury
gathering
to become the full moon shining on her turn towards me

o candle burn bright
for this is the night
when as she wakes up
she will see the whirling arrangement
of all the reflections in her eyes
in mine

73

if you love me any less
i will come down to earth and die

if you love me any less
i will proclaim the kingdom of loss

if you love me any less
i will break the heart of seasons

if you love me any less
i will debase the currency of promises

if you love me any less
i will devalue the meaning of words

if you love me any less
i will make worthless the comfort of dreams

if you love me any less
i will kill the magic of a big hug

if you love me any less
you would not have loved at all

74

thou hast not taken flight
      to that place in your heart
where the mind comes to rest from all the toil and toll of time
until you teach another soul to fly with you
until you give me wings
      and feel my body next to yours

then i will make thee a shade of my deeds
under which you can always mend your dreams
as they begin to burn on their way to the sun
then i will bring you back to me

thou doth take flight
and i love thee with all my free will

75

have you ever seen a monsoon drown itself
                in its own tears
have you ever seen a river take a bend
                and then vanish beneath the earth
have you ever seen the mime of clouds
                performing the dance of sails on lost ships
have you ever seen the distant glow of a lonely horizon
                turn into the neon shower of an artificial sky

have you ever seen the one you love cross the road during the rush hour
                looking back from the other side to find no one there
and see the reflection of mannequin love in the shop window
when there is nothing left to buy
and there is nothing you want to sell

have you ever seen the loved one
                with the eyes of the one you love
there are no reflections there
only you and what you want to see

76

life and death become meaningless
      in life without you
and in death
      for when it comes
all it will bring
      is the sense of life
you gave me

77

have you been to the other earth
      deep inside the mind of the universe
she too was born with the one you know
same history – same people – same dreams – same moment – same chaos –

have you seen us you and i
      looking at the same sky
wondering if we also exist on the other side of this reality
do you see me wanting to be with you
   here and now and in all dimensions
         of longing and surrender and care
can you not feel that you and I will always be one
on this earth that pains us so
and on the other that pains us so
on this mother earth that gives us our you and I
and on the other that gives us
      what we choose to make of this
our life together –

78

happy birthday

look back if you like
i am holding the earth in one hand
                    and your world in the other –

look here at this fall holding its breath
with sun-plated leaves saluting you with the gift of time –

look at yourself in the light of silent candles
each flame a companion to the other's shy dance
          begging you to celebrate the coming of age
of a deep deep happiness in a devil-may-care
                         amnesia of tomorrow –

look at your hands
          they are with such character
before all resplendent mirrors and illusions
and tell you what's in those silk-trapped boxes
                    even before you open them
while your fingertips hold back all the secrets of one promise
                         wrapping all your skies
with the cry from my heart –

remember
(you should know above all)
       some presents
need not be given to be received –

79

i was tiptoeing across her heart
afraid and gentle and tender
i did not want to burden her with my restlessness
and i heard her say
the heart is already yours
but the journey is ours –

80

let me tell you this:
if you do not have all the answers
   to all that you suffer
come to my heart
     and rest there
it is crowded
   with all the people you love
and in one corner
   i remain the one
who waits and waits –

81

you are my passion
you are my friend
you are my beginning
you are my end –

you are my first
you are my last
you are my thirst
you are my cast –

you are my sight
you are my want
you are my light
you are my haunt –

you are my mine
you are my mind
you are my shine
you are my find –

you are my reason
you are my sleep
you are my season
you are my deep –

you are my new
you are my old
you are my dew
you are my gold –

you are my day
you are my night
you are my stay
you are my flight

82

think of me
        when all around you
is not what you want
        but still have to see
        and labour through
                        happily –

remember this
        no matter how hard you try
you will never get what you want
        (one gets one and loses another)
and you may not want it when you do
but you will always want what you want –

where else will you find me
    if not in your heart and your mind and the surface of your body
how will you let me go when there is no need to do so
the inner recesses of mock freedoms are just as hollow
as the successes of social encounters with masks of hope
yet seem so full of promise signifying nothing –

think of me
and tell me it is the business of life
to love one so completely that all our tomorrows
are already lived in this one thought
despite all the noise of walking down the streets of the city

83

my ability to love you is not unlimited
              (you have to help me there)
capricious seasons of broken skies
waterfall monsoons hidden in shawls of pashmina clouds
your tears i hold as pearls in my oyster fears
life in a sand seashore
        strife in unloved answers
why do you cry out loud
           saying you don't understand
what is there to know when you hesitate to face
       the lament of yearning in an absent embrace
or the sheer abandon of belonging with all the freedom of your heart
or the passion that is enough to fulfil a thousand lifetimes
why bother to be afraid of all that has not happened
take an unkind fate and swirl it around the cosmos of our love
and then let the pundits read what they will
but if you ask me
      i know the answer
and if you have to have a question
        perhaps i should not even go to the answer

84

i forget the pain of other things
                  when i am with you
i forget the gains of make believe
                  when i am with you
i become the rain on thirsty springs
                  when i am with you
i remain enchained to questions of tomorrow
                  when i am with you
i smile in the answers of your trials
                  when i am with you
i regain the strength of your journey
                  when i am with you
i reclaim the desert in your fears
                  when i am with you
i call you to the valleys of evergreen hope
                  when i am with you
i stay all alone until you come alive
                  when i am with you
i am with you when you are not there
                  when i am with you
i am with you when i am with you
                  when i am with you

85

the night is always the love of my day
she becomes you in all the romance
      and the madness of the full moon
she covers the death of hard days
with the tender throw of star–begotten skies
and remains the mystery and the passion
   the day consumes as daily bread
in the office of sleepwalking survival –

the night is a friend only because you are
she brings the afterglow of your eyes
   as they close to rest in my heart
and this heart of mine burns a lighthouse
on diamond shores of treacherous waters
they appear so safe in the day
(to those who never want to walk on water)
but are the roof of a lost continent of longing
submerged in fears and betrayals
      and the alchemy of artificial gold
      and that ounce of happiness a new day
      thinks
      is left in the crucible –

the night is my freedom from the day
the night is when you are all free to be me
and I am shining in the reflected faith
     of your love –

86

the spirit and the flesh
hanker after you
waking or asleep
raindrops knocking on the window
way up on the clouds
and a filigreed horizon
paints the picture of
impressionist strokes of our hands
one guiding the other
the other become one

87

put me to sleep
you always say you will
but then you trace the wrinkles on my forehead
and whisper the stuff of stars
as the forecast of dreams
and the reality of foretold harvests
before a failed monsoon

lullabies of lust carry the night
        far into the meadows of doubt
it's gone too soon like the twisters of instinct
please don't hum and wish i turn on my side
and sweeten the tired eyes of a bad day with a rushed good-night

please stay and put me to sleep
but only if you have the courage to close your eyes or mine

88

if you can imagine
       your love for me
       is more beautiful
             than your beauty

and if you agree
i too am a party
not only to your sense of beauty
but also to the way you hijack
the look
and the turbulent breathing in
of all the clouds that seem dark
in their threat to become rain
just as i return home
           to find you again and again

89

show me the limit of your love
so that i don't cross
        uninvited
into the territory of prescribed contracts
and measured social existence

tell me i am mad
to seek your rule over my dreams
tell me i am stupid
        to feel ebb tides of life
on the shore where i live
with the ocean no one has yet named

90

i die poor
carrying dreams as tombstones
that weigh heavy upon blasé happy days
every unfulfilled turn around the corner
begs for an epitaph of fired wisdom
borrowed divinity
and all pretence of taking life seriously
impoverishes fate and then ultimately the last breath
calls out to you –

i die rich
    with my heart in your hands
with your words ushering in peace to my temple of faith
i have the eternal shade of your eyes
and thus i can count the blessings
of every kiss – each embrace
and taste all tears as the wine
that gives this love the ecstasy of caring
and the joy of not being afraid –

91

it is with reference to you
    that i slip out into the world
otherwise
    the building of my heart
needs just the scaffolding of your love
to survive the beating
of a harsh clime of a mind
    than can think of a world without you –

the only regular maintenance
             of my wear and tear
is the permanent visit of your love's labour
      to my heart's content –

metroliner

the hypnotic metre of the train's song is gone
the clippity-clop soothes you no more
the heart beats silently
   and the windows don't open to let the clouds in –

she has beautiful hands
   stuck to the keyboard of an awful computer
she is talking to herself while the green wall of trees
               passes her by
the coach vibrates with distant voices and churning wheels
and i hope so much she is talking to her loved one
      and not to the computer –

the train does not whistle any more
(that call of distant destinations half-travelled
         half-forgotten)
it just moans out the cry of a dead romance
the train does not carry a journey any more
it is the impersonal carriage of an unfeeling judgement –

i wonder if i would say all this if you were with me
would it matter that the track running beside my closed window
is a lonely companion to so many fixed eyes
would i care that the train has become a machine –

93

think in the alphabets of fire
(her eyes too command the flames of burning huts in my heart)
stare away the evil eye of temptress half-moon
and her reflection in the sea of sorrow
(is the full moon her sister too
          or is her planet not the earth
but a distant cousin of some forgotten fate)
think of her in the seal
                of the temple woman of the indus
gold and beauty and diamonds
and the enchantment of knowing
          that love is a sense of free will
in all the matrix of mere rocks and ether
think of her as the aesthetic of parthenon
gods and games
played in the rush to self-worship
all defeated
in her flourish of brave encounters with meaning
and in her silent dismissal
          of life's capricious bribes
she never took and never will
for i think of her
          and more often than not
she looks at me and says yes

94

she has a voice
   that carries the great songs
         of the slave years of jazz
and eases the pain no heroin can –
she lives in my heart's exile
         in the tribe of my dreams
and succumbs to the benign dictatorship of love
she the dictator
   she the citizen
she the arbiter
of the unwritten constitution of the state of blues –

she dances
with the hurricane grace of an andalusian flame
gypsy chants and wandering calls to passion
she has no compassion for the cowards who surrender
to the dregs of quotidian survival
she goes to war for the loved one
and brings back the victory of pure belonging –

95

tell me our love is good
tell me we are the balm of unspoken hurt
tell me we are anointed by our saints of passion
tell me we are one with the faith of our journey
tell me we'll never burn in the inquisition of doubt
tell me we will set each other free
tell me that freedom means nothing without the other
tell me the other is one step away from eternity
tell me it matters that time is sand
tell me we are the ocean that gathers
the lighted grains of our moments in life
and washes each one of them with the salt of our eyes –

96

the mind breaks
        into little prism pieces each
with self-beguiling answers across
   the entire spectrum of alien light –

the answers don't work
        and even if they do they
do not ask the questions that
   the heart has raised and
   found answers to:
in her presence in his look
in his belief in her love
in her knowledge of his peace
in his wealth of her promise
in her smile on his lips
in his account of her heart
in her shine in his care
in his words in her mind
in her mind in his heart –

97

why are all cliches true
        i love you
        i miss you
it's not cool to be blue –
why are all the pseudo emotions called real
i must live for myself and myself alone
self-sacrifice is unreal
        stupid
             uncool
what is in it for me
hold it
let me think about my very own self
one can always walk away
        get a new life
look back and pretend
        life is not a cliché
no point in endlessly saying i love you
        no gain in missing you
no acknowledgement of pain in any weak moment
that engulfs a whole life of just being in love –

98

the yards of muslin i weave for a living
can pass through a ring you wear when no one is there to see
what it means to own someone else's love so completely –
you need not worry about my sweat-soaked loom
it is a quaint affliction of the uncollected tolls of my heart's passage
that are now my savings draped in the veil you wear
to keep you from the world you do not create
and yet the muslin you pass through the ring
lets enough of the twinkle of many street lights
ignite the allure of being out there alone
make you believe in all there is you want –
so let me toil in cells of diaphanous walls
for i know i can almost breathe in this market-place
and not let you know the muslin you so love
has always been woven by my hands resting on your body
looking for the ring you wear when there is no one there but me –

99

love is the spectacle of faith
in the coliseum of the cruel city of time
every dream is a martyr to reality
each battle has to be won for the loved one
every stream of consciousness marvels at life
going upstream to spawn and die and live again –
love is the moment of glory
in the circus maximus of terracotta conquerors and real people
praetorian whims and real desires
clay ceasars and fragile gods
love is one look of the loved one
trembling for your life in the bloodthirsty crowd
love is one word that says yes to the magic
        of having chosen you
it is the celebration of all the freedom seized
    from all the salutations to death
love is –

100

if the wages of love are the currency of pain
pay me not in counterfeit wealth
let me be the richest man on earth
for i have toiled in my love for you
in nubian gold mines and lost rivers of the sahara
and have always come to rest in the cool camp of your embrace
please call off the whips of those who want to rule over us
let them not make us slaves stolen from masters of your own choice
i too am a slave but a happy one
i see you set me free
i see you smiling in the dignity of belonging
i see you distributing equal measures
          of olympian wine and mundane chores
and all i want to say is
here are the savings of joy
this is the vault of passion
the treasure is all yours –

101

you make the tea
from the richest leaves you pick
          from the slopes of darjeeling
you meet the gods in the foothills of the himalayas
and you beseech them to give your touch
the everlasting aroma of undying seasons of harvests
caught in the nectar of a perfect brew known only to you –
you fill your cupped hands
          with the alluvial gold of the great river that flows
under mother earth known only to you
and to all those who mould on the wheel of creation
turning with the speed of the unhurried whirl
          of your heart's dervishes
you make a cup so mud-like it glows in its own simplicity
you put it in the oven of true words
and you fill this cup with the tea you make
when you want to show your love –

102

she is my aesop's fable

there is a lesson in happiness

in all of life's madness

when she says, 'have blind faith in me

for all the calculus of rationality

for all the betrayals of self-interest

for all the fears of the fall

here are my arms

they are your wings of freedom

and my colossus of promise

to give you all the reasons you need to seek my body

and hold my heart' –

103

it's on the tip of my tongue

the poem so beautiful it came in a dream

i turned around to wake you

so that i could recite my dream and hold all the words in your body

you held out your hand in your sleep's wonderful smile

as if to say, 'yes, i know the dream, silly,

i sent the words to you

each a child of our love's craft

every word a prince of life's thesaurus' —

of all the dreams that make a poem

the one you plant in the mind's floating island

of the perpetual celebration of eternity

is the one that puts me to sleep

      and wakes me up —

104

you and i
    are that colour of the rain-washed sky
        stolen from a benign sun
which has no name
    and needs only the awe of our being together to see it –

when the day becomes the tender wish of your eyes
and your arms call night to their embrace
i weave moonbeams into the fabric of repaired care
and commit to memory the fragile patterns of all healing –

you and i
    are the happy knots of destiny
        braided into the silken shimmer of life
i long to open your hair
        for i know you'll sentence my fingers
to roam there in the joy of untangling poor fear
and just remain the heart
        on which you rest your head fearlessly –

you and i
    are that colour of the sky
everyone sees at the end of rain-soaked sunset
but only we can call our own –

105

this monsoon is dark and heavy
it takes the sky's blues
and brings to life the percussion of our heartbeat
with a dance of your pulse against mine
wrist upon wrist swaying in the waterfall of a happy season –
you don't have to see
           through the monsoon's filigree
you know i am there
           on the other side of the rain
the pain
           of not always clasping your outstretched hand
goes away as soon as you bring your part of the sky
and together we make sense of thundering clouds
reading out our kismet
with the tenderness of a breeze that covers your face
after the rain –

106

how far does the river of ache flow into the heart
how much does the delta of pain resemble
        my stretched-out hand
this palm – these lines
the tributaries of fate watering
an oasis of my thirst for you
in which a full moon comes down to live in its own reflection –

how can you not wonder at the freedom being in love gives
how can you pretend then to go about your way in another world
where the nitty-gritty of being unaware
    brings only the urgency of time lost
searching for the sun in a sky populated by
uncaring clouds
and untraced silhouettes
        of half-remembered stencils of all our images
    kept locked in your eyes –

107

it's no good
this bread and butter you put on my table
i too can put my hand in the oven of mundane hunger
and pull out a loaf of survival
these pearls and diamonds you grind
       to make me a tonic
give me an illness only you can cure
so please
stay with me and let me earn you
       the wages of love
let me show you the wealth of my eyes
       the feast of my sighs
let me not doubt for once
what you are to me
what i am to you
let me bake you an island
       from the bread of my body
and let me be with you
when you are with me –

108

in the forgotten pocket of a torn velvet coat
i found these words that had been lost
                  on the way to a poem
the velvet had dried in the seasons of affluence
and my dress got mended again and again
                  with the stitches of poverty
but these words kept on hiding and hoping
                  to find the poem they so wanted to create –

so what does it take to make a poem:
not words in the plenty of their meaning
                  alone in resplendent rhyme
nor in the shine of a moon full of beauty
not music that pulls out the heart's chords
and sets to melody only what the words can hear
no not any perfection of thought
nor a fancy nobility of any metaphor –

there is no poem without you
there is no word that can join another
without your glance that comes my way
there is no magic in the dance of alphabets
and there is no coming together of all these words
unless you turn around and raise all of them as our children
and save them from just the meaning they have –

109

how many colours of the sky have you seen
how many clouds have stolen the tapestry of your heart
how many rainbows have betrayed the secrets of light and rain
how many words have you spoken that i have not called mine
how many smiles have you kept hidden from yourself
how many times have you asked the mirror who's the bravest of them all
how many times have you closed your eyes and found me within
how many times have you seen tears of joy and tears of sadness in one drop of time
how many times have you looked back and found me waiting
how many times have you carried me across the anger of life's flood
how many times have you saved me from not wishing at all
how many times have you wondered if you have a choice
how many times have you chosen me again and again
how many times have you thought why it matters
how many times
how many times —

110

you
and the idea of you
are the same
that
is love –

111

the wake of your look
shakes my gaze upon your sail-eyes
carrying the cargo of freely traded love
and the flotilla of my dreams
rocks merrily with each wave born of your journey
to bring back to me the untold treasures
of the other side of the unknown –

112

this place you have come to
       is my heart
your windows my eyes
the door you closed behind you
       is the gateway to a whole continent of love
the sadness you bring on lonely wings
will leave you
when you let yourself back in the company
of the one who never left
and never will

113

this parchment – this skin –
the body of the lioness that gathers all my dreams
and renews the garment of her strength
in helping me see the words as they are born –
i sow all alphabets of all languages i know
scripts of fear – abandonment – lonely saharas
      of beaten caravans
a sense of a writer's hand lying buried in the sand
half-composed stanzas of trapped music waiting to be sung
i weed out the false gods of sand temples
and obscure hymns faking discovery in my own mirage
i begin to write
and while the poetry shines out in hidden rhyme
i run out of ink
the parchment is dry
and my ink-blood flows into an oasis
that was watered long long ago by all my tears –

114

say yes
even if the scales of self-interest say no
say i will go
          eyes closed
across broken bridges and burning rivers
and give you the faith you think i waiver in
          when the song of time becomes
too discordant and distant –
say yes
          this love is difficult
but no more than earning bread
    or falling ill or running out of tomorrow
yes
i am what makes us all complete
yes
you are the one who carries me
          across broken bridges and burning rivers –

115

o happy whispers
carried by the bride breeze
      giving music to thoughts
you have barely let be known to yourself:
can i add softly to what you are saying
can i say i understand why sadness
      stays with the journey of carnival love –

i am going to breathe in your voice
and let it make me hear why it's all right
to learn to see in the dark
to burn your fingertips to save the candles
      when the sun is out
to turn to the dancing warmth of your eyes
as they light up the crackle
in the fireplace of my heart –

o happy whispers
      stay
and repeat yourself in the joy of the bride breeze
and the vows of a celebration that goes on and on

116

now i sleep
          with dreams – the artists of the mind
they bring you to me
          with the vigour of the renaissance
each thought a turning-point of faith
every shimmer an illumination of your candle eyes –

i always start as the master of my dreams
and i always slip into the garments of truth
you stitch with the threads of pain and illusion
i always sleep with you beside me
and i am the one who falls into an ocean of words
you help me sail through on your ship
that always reaches the shore of promises
leaving behind all the terrible storms
and all the shipwrecks of lament –

117

in your love
        time
the jailer of life
        becomes a friend
and gives leave of absence
        from the solitary confinement
of a hurried sentence of memories
        in the cellar of meaningless survival –

in our love
        there is this castle of belonging
guarded by this space only we can see
in which every room has a heart
and all windows have eyes
    that are yours
        and yours alone –

118

it flows in your veins
it is a drop of pure dew on scorched lips
it is the stuff of memories just a moment old
it is the harvest of golden thoughts in the land of sighs
it is the spoils of war against fear and weary hope
it is the look of aphrodite as she becomes mortal for you
it is the sense of sadness and the arresting fragility of laughter
it is the way you say i don't know
it is the armour of dreams protecting sleep
it is the peace of rest when tired bodies go out to work
it is letting the sun and the moon go free
it is spinning the earth in the palm of your hand
it is when i flow in your veins
it is when you become the life of my blood –

119

every written word embellishes reality
each spoken one bemoans the trap of meaning
every change of season captures the turning of the heart
each branch of a sad tree carries the blossom of tomorrow –

so now dear one
send me a letter i'll read again and again
and feel i am the words falling from your fingertips
call me and say there is nothing to worry about
let nothing trap us with unsaid lament
i want your heart to send me a sweet breeze
in the thick of humid absences
let me see the blossom in your eyes
give me the fragrance of untapped nectars
of our love.

120

you are my dreamful peaceful sleep

you are the breath that watches over me

you are the way out of this city deep

you are the stealth in the look that is mine

you are the smile in a crowd that distracts fate

you are the balm of whispers in the noise

you are the song i always sing in the humdrum

you are the current that fuels my imagination

you are the puzzle that unfolds into a solution

you are the oracle of my temple of time

you are the secret path into the realm of the ordinary

you are the open road to every olympus there is

you are the hand that holds my hand

you are the one who is my stand

you are the one who says yes

you are the one who is and remains –

121

why complicate a simple truth
        i love you beyond the sunrise
              and the moonglow
pity those who want to measure
        the angle of sunrays falling on their eyes
or the milligrams of joy in every moonbeam

why worry when your heart is always mine
why complain to the stars when all it takes
        for the entire constellation to smile
is a mere whisper to yourself
a happy refrain saying how much
your love sets you free –

122

a poor man falls in love
        breaks his heart
becomes rich
        loses all passion
cannot find his way home
and forgets the language of a woman's eyes –

he sees her again
        everywhere he looks
he crosses his desert
and waits by the shore of his once alive ocean
he looks back and suddenly says to himself:
she has to be all the wealth there is
she has to be what was once rich about me
she remains my ocean of healing
she is what life has given me –

123

every time i think of you
        the fall moon comes out to fill the hollows
            of your absence
and the sun stays with me
            just a little longer at dusk
to warm my heart with the golden light
            of your presence in my pulse –

every time i think of you
        i rush through life's wonders
great and small
children mine and children yours
bread-winning chores
          and the sheer luck of having you on my side –

think of all that can go wrong with us
think of all the cruel twists of fate
and then share some of the laughter
        of the gods with me
and believe
and have faith
and make this love
        the be all and end all of just one moment –

124

do you hear me in the crowd of all your lament
am i really your ally against the curses of destiny
do you hold me dear when you are sad
would you believe there is no nirvana
do you know there are no answers
can you let go of all the safety harnesses
      they will not save you from the fall
unless you have faith in me
will you not then want to fly
      in the wake of freedom this love is all about
is it possible that these words are more than words
do you really think you can love me enough
or will you one day stop and cry
enough –

125

in all my days of waiting and searching
there was a light that shone and played games with me
i thought it was you
it was
and is but i did not know
till in all the steps i took in sand
i saw the signs of how your eyes
would always be the breeze and the shade
and how in every mirage
the oasis of your embrace
would be as real as the first drop of water
after all the dry years of the great wait . . .

in all my days that have gone by
in all my nights orphaned by a heartless moon
in all my dreams more real than hope
i have always known that you are the wait
i have always known that you are the search
i have always felt you the hand
that holds my wrist . . .

126

i love you – just think
how much; how with
the fullness of my being; how
total; how brave; how
helpless; how happy in the
feeling that i can give you
some happiness –

127

come to think of it
i love you enough
to write at least one poem
that will not die before my love
or feel the music of my senses
known and unknown
till my ashes fall on sacred rivers
and cleanse death of its threat
or just not give a damn
and walk straight into
every forbidden corner of your heart
and like a homeless traveller on rich pavements
lay claim
to every parchment of lament
and turn it into satin scrolls of life
even the pharaohs could not possess –

128

say something
   not
of this fear
   this pain
   this fear
that falls on open wounds

or say nothing
but don't let me go
and just tell the world
   to go away
or give us the time
   to stay together
beyond words –

129

of the infinite steps of her heart
i climbed
but a step or two
while she kept my heart
in the palm of her hand
and came down and said
do not count the steps
for each one
is worth a thousand lifetimes —

130

only a heartache can cure a heartache
only the brave fall in love
only her arms can ease the pain
only her freedom gives me life

only the sun can see her eyes
only the moon can shine on her
only her aura can make me see
only a phoenix can live her fire

only a dream can beget a dream
only her quietude of the heart has melody
only she can walk up to altars of her own making
only she has vows of the four seasons
       and all the planets of my heart

131

make this night
an oven
to bake an embrace
that parts only
to seek the other in you
or your own reflection in me —
enough

132

sad how the prisoners of time
live in the prison of the future
sad how the present is dead
even before it becomes the past

133

when you are tired of sitting on the fence
when you feel fulfilled by a given social contract
when sons and daughters go their own way
when the workday is a bitch between the home and the office
when friends of yore glean the skirmishes of life off you
when the trapeze of remembrance swings by a face in the crowd
when one love is the entire thesaurus of your own language

134

be warned o happy one
beneath every smile that passes your way
there is the highway of grief
for every dream that comes true
there is one
       just that one
the one that recurs in your sleep
       and in every dawn
and it is the one that then leaves you

135

'between what i see and i say

between what i say and what i
keep silent

between what i keep silent and
what i dream

between what i dream and what i
forget:

poetry.'

octavio paz

136

you don't cry about death
        you just die
so come life
let us forsake the epitaphs and eulogies of
            betrayed memories
and write the diary of every moment
hand in hand

137

if you want an average love
then you want nothing
for averages know nothing of pain
and remain the measure of mediocrity

138

where are the companions of my madness
where are the priests of passion
where are the sacred chants of salvation
where are the soldiers of beauty
where are the guardians

139

and so this wave of sadness has returned to its home, way down in the depths of the sea. thanks to the tireless ocean mariner who tends to her tides with vast amounts of love, ample enough to overcome all of her storms.

and so this ocean carries her sadness deep within
her life-giving waters, all streams, all
currents flow back to her cleansed by the
dissolved salt of tears no one sees except
the one she loves, he tells her there are no
tears in this love, just the salt of loyalty,
passion and soul-warming desire; just the
taste of corporeal lust only she commands;
and just the odyssey of abandonment and
belonging that needs no lighthouse for this
embrace of ours is the only epic that
we understand; the only eternity that
matters —